Transmission

You are about to enter a dark new world.

Forget everything you think you know.

Open your mind.

Take everything in.

Dare to read between the lines.

Dare to come face to face with your deepest fears.

Remain strong in mind.

Don't forget to act brave.

This is Total Eclipse Of The Sun.

Act I – The Arsonist

Rain falls steadily down on three fresh graves.

The names on them read Tina, Damien and Maria Staves.

Taken before their time was set to expire,

their deaths left a hole in me no one should admire.

Forsaken by the one I gave my life to,

I now curse his name and sip away on brew.

Tears fall from my eyes, they never remain dry.

I sit in front of the graves and let out a sigh.

I wish I wasn't so weak,

I wish my life didn't seem so bleak.

No longer do I sport a strong physique,

gone is the trait that made me unique.

The pain that consumes me is too great to bear.

My demise is written in stone I swear.

If I hadn't been forsaken I would say a prayer,

but when I need you the most you're no longer there.

I'm left in a state of despair, left alone to rot.

Right next to their graves is my very own plot.

I'd rather be there then on a yacht.

Life's a bitch at least I gave it a shot.

The sun shines through the windows as I take my place,

behind the podium I'm reminded of God's loving grace.

My family is front and center, they are every Sunday morning.

Their constant presences I find so warming.

My son reminds me of his mother, blonde hair and blue eyes

dressed in a shirt and tie he looks ready to rise.

Great things I know he's capable of

I just wish he would smile more and share his love.

My daughter takes after me, her eyes big and brown.

When I stare into them I can never frown.

She's the head cheerleader, popular as one can be.

One day she will leave and be free

to spread her wings and be a success.

She gives me no reason to stress.

My wife, beautiful, strong and bold,

her smile warms me up when life has me cold.

I feed off her strength, it fuels my passion

to spread the love of God even though religion is going out of fashion.

We were childhood friends, now a life-long pair,

created two offspring to be our heirs.

She's the best friend I have always had,

even when I was a loser who wore plaid.

My family is the constant image I always see

as I stand in front of the congregation tall as a tree.

I open my mouth and speak

good morning (good morning).

Hiding in a corner chewing off her finger nails,

fear shivers down her spine her face is pale.

Darkness surrounds her she's home all alone,

yet she feels completely out of her zone.

The phone lines and power have been cut off.

She's sick with a cold but too afraid to cough.

An evil laugh echoes throughout the dark of the house.

Tears fall from her eyes she feels smaller than a mouse.

The hairs on her arms stick straight up like static.

The man she loves is hunting for her, shit's about to get climatic.

"Whore" echoes throughout the home.

"Whore" roles off his tongue, at his mouth he foams

you fucked with the wrong man my dear!

Now the life you took for granted is shifting into another gear.

I will punish you for your betrayal and it will be severe!

Your future no longer seems so clear!

Crouching in a corner she comes in contact with his eyes,

sees a demon but is not surprised.

She saw it in his eyes every time he was high,

but decided to ignore it and believe her own lies

that things would change and get better.

Her belief in him has now made her his debtor.

He places his hand over her mouth and whispers in her ear,

"you shouldn't have betrayed me and rode another man's spear.

You always thought I was insane but you had no idea.

Now you're going to witness the devil inside me Mia."

Screams of agony echo throughout the house

as Mia is tied up and doused

in gasoline and set on fire.

Burned alive is the way she retires.

The smell of burned flesh enters his nostrils, brings him glee.

His dark deed is done time to flee

and cover up the evidence of his crime.

Pride overcomes him he feels so sublime.

He douses the home in gasoline and sets the place ablaze.

But he's taken too long; exits the house to waiting police who are not amazed.

Phase one is complete, he surrenders without a fight.

His future is now clear and bright.

Sitting at a table across from his own son,

he searches for words to begin a conversation but finds none.

Disbelieve at his sons heinous actions has him in shock.

His son stares into his soul waiting to mock.

Tears overcome him as he mumbles "I love you."

"You love God for that you will rue."

"You're my son I loved you more."

"Don't lie I was nothing to you but a chore."

"God forgives you; he loves you like his very own son.

Let him in and he will show you the sun,

take you away from the darkness you are lost in.

I know you are a good person, where has he been?"

"Your faith blinds you father there is no God!

You worship a book written by man that's flawed.

I'm the living proof the bible is a lie.

Do me a favor and look up to the sky,

ask yourself how a 'loving God' can create me,

a monster that set his girlfriend on fire in glee?"

"The Devil has corrupted your soul,

stealing the weak from God is his goal.

See through his deceit and find your way back to the light.

It's not too late to make everything right."

"Stop is already father; I set bibles on fire for fun!

I belong to Lucifer and my deed for him is done.

He expects both of us in the wreckage father!

Give up on God; he's not worth the bother."

"Why did you kill Mia son?

She was an amazing girl, energetic and fun.

She never wronged you and yet you end her life?

You loved her and wanted her to be your wife."

"Why did Jared Lee Loughner shoot Gabrielle Giffords in the head?

Why did James Eagan Holmes shoot up a theatre and dye his hair red?

For the same reason Damien Allen Staves set Mia on fire.

Too gather media attention that will help other lost souls aspire

to create chaos and fear in a world blinded by a fake God!

And expose the lies fed to us by people like you, a fraud!

I am Leviathan an agent of chaos dad.

I have shaken your world at its very foundation, I'm so glad.

Your faith is in doubt; I see it in your eyes.

You're beginning to think, 'maybe I'm not so wise.'

The son you claim to love, you now despise...

...and I detest the fact that I was baptized.

The storm is just beginning for you.

I will destroy your soul like you destroy mine when you spew your lies to hundreds of souls week after week.

You thought your future was bright now it's awful bleak."

"You are not the son I raised and know.

It destroys me I will no longer be able to watch you grow.

Despite what you think you will not break my faith.

You will become nothing more to me than a wraith.

I will love you until the very end

and hold onto faith that God will save you and help you mend.

Goodbye son I hope one day you will again be my friend."

"See you in the fire father; your fall will be fast and hard.

Your perfect little life has now been marred!"

Lost in a deep sleep my mind still racing,

contemplating a life without the son I never considered replacing.

His words from the day before still sting and hurt,

I have to remain strong I can't let him drag me into the dirt.

The phone rings my eyes shoot open I'm awake.

The caller I.D. reveals the informant, my heart begins to break.

I pick up the phone and press it against my ear.

I hope for the best but I'm overcome with fear.

"Mr. Staves this is Officer Briggs we need you to come to the jail.

I'm sorry sir we tried our best but to no avail.

Your son took his own life last night.

I warn you it's not a pleasant sight.

He left behind a note addressed to you.

You might not want to read it but it might be a clue

to why he ended his life.

I suggest you also bring your wife."

I hang up the phone with my heart now sunk,

my hands shake as I wake up my wife.

Tears explode from my eyes "our son ended his life!"

I hug her saying, "we need to go down to the jail,

he left behind a note," my face goes pale.

"I hope this letter finds you well,

by well I mean burning in the fires of Hell.

Total Eclipse Of The Sun

Since you are reading this you know I'm dead.

My only regret, not being there when you receive the call and witness your eyes fill with dread.

I've gone to a far better place, far away from my own personal Hell.

The Hell you helped to create I remember the day well.

I was just a little boy back then

when I was violated by your very close friend!

Over the next couple years that one time became a trend.

I was too weak to even defend

myself from his advances you can't even comprehend

the betrayal I felt when no one would listen to my cries!

Even you thought I was full of lies!

I was viewed as nothing more than a faggot!

But I had the last laugh against that maggot.

I bit off his dick then set it on fire!

As he screamed in agony, this was the first time I began to aspire.

With the help of my friends, those voices in my mind,

I realized the truth and saw just how blind

you were and made everyone else by the lies you spewed

as you preached the fake word, how so crude.

My friends opened my eyes and helped me to elude

the lies you sold and continue to sell twelve years later.

You're a criminal far worse than a traitor.

For my words you need no translator.

My heart was filled with hate, that's how I know there is no creator.

He would never have caused me to suffer all these years.

At least in the end I no longer fear

but welcome death because I'm already in Hell!

Now I'm off so I will no longer dwell

on this useless planet living this pointless life.

I don't want a wife, I long for the knife.

I slit my wrists in vain; sign this letter with my blood,

leave you to be with this thud,

words written by the wise man Tyler.

I hope they inspire you like they did me."

"You're now lost in my jungle welcome to Hell.

This is the place where there is no law for me to dwell.

My body is covered in the blood of a rabbit.

This is no place for you to inhabit.

Ahead of you, behind you and beside you, you notice me,

with a twisted smile across my face you have nowhere to flee.

You close your eyes tight and pray to be saved.

I slit your throat quick and watch you gasp for your last breaths.

Searching through the chambers of my mind,

do you like what you see or do you go blind?

Keep searching through the abyss I call my world.

Inside lays the key, keep searching for that's the key."

Damien

Back home from the jail we sit in silence

with the images of our sons slit wrists burned into our minds.

Images that make us wish we were blind.

I look at my wife, her strength I hope to find.

Her facial expressions are overcome with grief,

she forces a smile but it's only brief.

Damien's death and letter have left us in disbelief.

Tina gets up and puts her arms around me,

puts her mouth to my ear then counts to three.

"It's not your fault our son went mad,

you're a great father you should be glad.

Damien blamed you for his own issues.

I know it hurts, here take some tissues."

"I hate Mathew for molesting our son."

"But he's in jail for the sins he's done."

"I need a drink, something to help me relax."

"Alcohol won't help take away the axe

that you feel in your spine…

…I also feel it in mine."

"My son is a murderer, killed himself and blames it on me."

"People blame others for their decisions so they can be free

of the guilt that comes along with making those choices.

Our son was mad, tormented by voices."

I get up, go into the kitchen and take out a drink.

Pour it into a glass and down it before I can blink.

Driving down the road rain gently taps on the roof.

The night time sky is black, starless with no moon.

I hit on a joint as I pass a saloon.

I love weed it brings me out of my cocoon.

I pass the joint to Mia she takes a large hit.

Chokes and coughs since she's a rookie but won't admit.

I scan the area for a dark alley.

Mia knows what I'm up to and disagrees verbally.

I pull into an alley and shut off the car,

pull a bag out of my pocket that's straight from Dakar.

I cut up a line and inject it straight into my brain,

no longer do I experience pain.

Mia shakes her head in disapproval of my action.

I see fear in her eyes, it's my main attraction.

I slap her across the face tell her not to criticize me.

"I wish you would stop" she pleas.

Mia rubs her nose as blood drips from it.

The animal inside me rattles its cage it will not submit.

It wants to hunt and feast on fear.

It hunts for pray far more dangerous than deer.

I exit the car and begin walking down the street.

Mia runs after me begging me to retire with her to her suite.

The animal has been unleashed, it's hardened like concrete.

She sees the beast in my eyes and says she's tired of my deceit.

I back hand her, she falls to the ground hard.

Her soul has been shattered like glass, her heart charred.

She gets up and says she's going over to John's.

Says he's the gold medal winner and I take home the bronze.

I cuss her out and promise she will pay.

She will not leave me alone, lost in gray.

She says we are through and doesn't care if I fray.

You will pay dearly Mia Marie Cay.

Boiling with rage I spot a homeless man across the street.

I go up to the man and ask him if I can buy him something to eat.

"That would be very kind of you young man."

I deliver a knuckle sandwich and begin to carry out my plan.

I deliver punch after punch to his face.

He's a disgrace to the human race.

He begs for me to stop, instead I pick up the pace.

Your mistake believing I was full of grace.

I deliver a kick to his head then stop the assault.

His face is a bloody wreck, his own damn fault.

His breathing stops, I turn and walk away,

turn my attention to Mia, She's the buffet.

Every night I sleep alone wondering what has happened

to the man I love, you're not the same man.

We have drifted apart, that wasn't part of our plan.

We wanted to marry and raise a big clan.

When I look into your eyes I no longer see good.

I see anger, hate and unbelievable pain I have never understood.

You take your built up anger out on me,

and blame your father that shouldn't be.

I was with you the day you changed.

I looked into your eyes and saw a man deranged.

You lost your idol that day, the man you love,

but he's still with you just from up above.

This is the day you became devoid of faith

and the memories of your grandpa became a wraith.

You witnessed your hero fall to his death.

The shock of that moment took away your breath.

The pain of his demise tore you apart at the seams.

I know you wish it was just a dream.

After his death, when I looked into your eyes,

the monster I saw took me by surprise.

Anger and hate consume your soul.

It has hardened you with a constant darkness and left you spoiled.

Four months later you're like a man I never knew.

To this day I'm afraid of you.

I pray for you to let go of all the hate,

so we can forget the past and start on a new slate.

However every day that passes my hope for us dims.

I'm beginning to believe I'm better off wrapped in someone else's limbs.

You're destroying yourself and it's tearing me apart!

You act like I'm unimportant, do you have no heart?

I fear the day you take your rage out on me.

Maybe then I will realize we are not meant to be.

I wish I could talk to you and open your eyes

but you won't listen to my cries.

Maybe if I leave for John you will get the point,

I'm more important to you than your joints.

It's a shame what you have become,

but what do I know you would sell me out for rum.

Mia – Journal entry 42

Sitting around the kitchen table playing cards,

Rummy is the game, and when I win again I'll send my regards.

I play with my grandpa he's the hero I aim to be.

I'm told I'm great but I disagree.

I will never be able to carry on his legacy

since I suffer from a disease that's decaying my chemistry.

Playing cards with him allows me to be at peace.

I use it as a release

to escape my feelings for a period of time

and allow myself to focus on my rhymes.

Being raped as a child scarred my mind.

I wish I could escape my past and leave it behind,

but my life is no longer aligned.

Courtesy of playing cards I'm given a chance to unwind.

Those were the days I still held some control.

I watched my hero die, an event that left a hole

through my heart and through my soul.

Now I medicate with a bowl,

and my eyes burn with anger like coal.

My relationship with Mia has not been the same.

It doesn't help that she refuses to share the blame,

and it doesn't help that the voices fuel the flame.

I'm fighting a war not playing a game.

Mia could try to not look at me in shame.

I'm losing my mind and going insane.

My soul is constantly dumped on by rain.

I'm a changed man not for the better.

Even though I said in my letter

I would remain strong until I see you again,

I'm telling you right now in pen,

I'm breaking apart and losing control.

Total Eclipse Of The Sun

My mind is shattered, no longer a whole.

Time to blow off steam and go for a stroll.

You were my best friend, not just a brother.

I will miss you daily, you are my brother I will never have another.

I wish I would have known how troubled you were.

My time spent with you seems like a blur.

I never knew you were so messed up in the head.

The smile you always gave me, I was so mislead.

You hid your demons well.

I wish you would have came out of your shell

and shared your issues with me.

I have issues too; I just want to be free

from the hell I'm in, it's the reason I cut.

It helps me feel like I'm less of a nut.

But now you're gone and I'm left alone

to fight my inner issues that swarm like a cyclone.

I will continue my war in hopes of making you proud.

I know you're not below me but up in the clouds.

I know you are not a monster, just a lost soul.

Winning my war is my own personal goal.

I'm strong like mom,

so I won't explode like a bomb.

I will remain focused and calm.

Rest in peace brother I will see you again soon.

<u>Act II – Taboo</u>

Rain continues to fall as I stare at the graves.

The names are enhanced by the rain, Damien, Tina and Maria Staves.

I'm left alone in a world that is cold.

I wish I could smile but all I do is scold.

A bible has been placed by the grave of Tina.

Attached to it is a note from her friend Nina.

I pick up the bible and throw it.

God I no longer worship, on God I quit!

I hung up my robe and walked away from the church.

I walked to the forest and sat under a birch.

From there I began my search.

The search for an answer to the question, why was I abandoned by God?

Taking my place in front of the church I feel at home.

God provides me with strength inside his dome.

My foundation has been shaken but I aim to remain strong.

I'm looking to move forward, I know the journey will be long.

My wife is back in the front row

smiling at me to help me through this low.

The church needs its pastor to grow.

I will not bow to the Devil below.

My daughter is sitting next to her mother.

I read pain on her face from losing her brother.

I have faith in her to pull through after this loss,

just like I have faith that Jesus died for us on the cross.

The spot next to Maria is empty and cold.

The congregation views it as a place to scold.

The spot will remain empty for years to come

since no one dares to enter the slum.

It's a forbidden place viewed as evil by some.

I open my bible and take a deep breath,

look over at my acolyte Beth.

Begin the service with a cheerful good morning.

The smile on my face tells you a lie.

Inside I'm broken, lost in darkness, begging to cry.

Craving for weed because I live my life high.

People believe I'm happy but really I'm sly.

Mirror, mirror on the wall, who's the biggest slut of them all?

I am it makes me feel so small.

I whore myself out in hopes to feel tall!

It leaves me broken, through mud I crawl.

The mirror on my wall is my worst damn enemy.

I'm ugly as sin no matter how beautiful my peers tell me endlessly.

"You look like the models I see in all those books."

I look like a worn down criminal because I'm nothing more than a crook.

I believe I'm fat no matter how thin I get.

Even though I'm head cheerleader and do the splits,

I never satisfied with my need to be fit.

I need help I will admit.

My father believes I will be successful and strong.

My friends believe I've been destined for greatness all along.

I'm a failure at life that will amount to nothing.

I'm a waste of space on this planet called Earth.

I piss away the day lighting up my bowl,

then I wonder why inside me there is a hole.

I wish I wasn't a pot head but I'm out of control,

being dead inside takes its toll.

I continue to fight the depression destroying my soul.

I'm too strong for my own good I wish I would just roll

over and give up the fight since the war can't be won.

But I will fight until black is the color of the sun.

Maria - Journal entry 192

Standing in front of my brother's grave I can't help but cry.

He left far too soon, I'm not ready to say goodbye.

I hope you are looking over me from the sky

wearing your Sunday shirt and tie.

You always looked handsome I will not lie.

Why wasn't it my death that was nigh?

Amanda hugs me tight from behind, whispers in my ear

"he will always be watching over you, you have no need to fear."

Kisses me on the lips, smiles and says, "my dear

you will always have me let's make that clear."

Kisses me again, this time slipping me tongue.

I pull away like I was just stung.

"Not here Amanda we can't be seen!

Let's get out of here and smoke some green.

My parents would kill me if they found out I was gay,

disown me and force me away."

"Maria my love we have no need to hide.

Your parents will understand and won't be a divide.

We are a couple in love and should show it with pride!

We can take the world's hate in stride."

"Amanda you're right, my parents I will tell.

I just hope they take the news well.

Don't instantly damn my soul to Hell

because that is a place I never want to dwell."

Total Eclipse Of The Sun

Amanda smiles and thanks me with a kiss

for the bravery she believes I contain that has always been amiss.

I would rather have my soul damned to the abyss

then miss out on a life with Amanda in bliss.

Craving weed we sneak off into a nearby forest,

pack up a bowl to get nice and high.

Amanda winks at me ready to comply.

I love getting high with her I won't deny.

Twenty minutes later I feel like I can fly.

Amanda is sitting next to me acting innocent and shy.

I give her a kiss; she pushes me to the ground.

Her aggression catches me off guard but leaves me astound.

She smiles into my eyes and slowly unzips my pants.

Takes them off and throws them onto some plants.

She grabs my thong with her teeth and pulls them off my body.

Sticks her tongue between my legs I feel disembodied.

My breathing becomes heavy as I drift off…

Three in the morning I still can't sleep.

My mind is restless, I feel like a black sheep.

Telling my parents the truth has me stressed,

but my homosexuality needs to be addressed.

I pace around my room pulling at my hair,

my mind is a mess, not like anyone cares.

There are times I wish I wasn't gay but that's not fair.

I love Amanda, should be proud of it and just not care

what others think, they can judge me from their chairs.

My head hurts it just won't stop spinning.

I swear being in a taboo love is worse than sinning.

I need something for my head to take away the ache,

it's times like these I wish I was baked.

It helps relieve the stress of being awake.

I hate being sober, it makes me want to break.

I enter the bathroom to check the medicine cabinet for pills.

My mom always has a stash I use to get my fill.

I open the cabinet find a stash of valium, I can't help but smile.

Nice stash mom, this is my style.

I take eight pills, close the cabinet door.

Turn around, spot myself in a mirror and think what a whore.

I don't understand how people find me attractive; I'm such an ugly bore.

I use to think highly of myself but that was before

depression took over and dropped me to the floor.

I return to my room with the valium in hand.

I take all eight in hopes of drifting off to an alternate land.

Tomorrow is the day I will most likely be banned,

since I play with fruit and not with sand,

reveal to my parents my ultimate plan.

Sitting in my desk listening to my teacher talk,

the blackboard behind her is littered with chalk.

Outside a ship is traveling through the lock,

time stands still as I stare at the clock.

In front of me sits a girl, her hair long and brown.

She keeps looking back at me but when she does I look down.

She's the prettiest girl in the entire town.

I wonder what she looks like in a night gown.

I don't know why I'm attracted to her, it doesn't seem right.

I love her eyes, they sparkle nice and bright.

I really like her I should ask her for a name,

however she's a girl they are all the same.

They laugh at me and think I'm lame

because I'm not attracted to boys, that I proclaim.

The teacher called on her, her name is Amanda.

Easy enough to remember my cousin is named Miranda.

I really want to talk to her but I'm much too shy.

My parents preach man and woman so I guess I should comply.

Sitting around the kitchen table dinner has just begun.

I can tell my father is hurting over his son.

He's dead silent, looks down and defeated.

I have a feeling shit is about to get heated.

I'm sorry but the truth can no longer be secreted.

I pray everyone will remain seated.

I look at my father, smile at him to catch his eye.

Look at my mother who's addicted to valium and already high.

Here goes nothing it's do or die!

I hope I hold it all together, don't break down and cry.

"I have a confession to make, a secret I've kept for some time.

I'm in love and it feels sublime,

but my love is for Amanda, we're currently dating.

I've been reluctant to tell you, afraid you would resort to hating."

"You're my daughter I support any decision you make.

I know telling us this wasn't a piece of cake.

I can't speak for your father, but I support you.

I just hope you thought this decision through."

"It's not a choice I made; it's not my choice to be gay!

I feel like it's a curse damning me to fray!

But I will no longer hide in the gray!

I love Amanda, the consequences I'm willing to pay.

I look at my father, his face has turned red.

I read pain on his face, inside he might actually be dead.

"Do you still love me dad?

I'm sorry I didn't fall in love with Chad.

I know you think the world of him and him plus I would make you glad.

However I love Amanda…I can tell you're mad."

"I could say I'm disappointed but that's an inaccurate claim.

You were the one meant to carry on the Staves name.

I don't know what's going on in your head but trust me it's a game!

Your 'love' for Amanda is nothing more than a flame.

Homosexuality is a sin defined by the bible.

I could tell you I support you but then I would be libel

for committing the sin of lying.

Don't look at me like you are about to begin crying!

Love can be tough when called for!

I don't want my daughter to be known as a whore!

Who spreads her legs like an open door,

and screwing the same sex is the only way she scores!"

"Thank you father I expected nothing less from you.

I'm a disappointment in your eyes, I know it's true.

The bible misleads you dad,

try not to be sad.

God is the one who made me gay,

just like he made night and day.

Believe me I wish I could say my love was named Ray.

However it's not, it's Amanda and she's here to stay!"

"I love you Maria don't ever believe I don't

but homosexuality is a choice, you're not made gay.

You're not following the bible, you're beginning to stray.

I hope you wake up and realize the truth

you choose to be gay because it's cool with the youth."

"Damien would understand and support me dad.

I wish so much he wouldn't have gone mad."

"Don't you dare bring your brother into this!"

"Sorry dad I know it hurts but sometimes love hurts!

Please just understand me, I'm not asking you to convert.

Just accept me for who I am

I will prove you homosexuality is not a scam."

"I'm done discussing this tonight Maria."

"Fine dad I'm going to Amanda's I need to relax.

I need to be with someone who has my back

and doesn't try to break it with an axe."

"You went too hard on her Steve.

Give her a chance and try to believe

that she knows what she's trying to achieve.

Don't give her a reason to leave."

"I will never accept her being gay

but I will try to go easy on her and not force her to stray."

Relaxing in bed, wrapped in Amanda's arms I'm beginning to feel right.

Stress was tearing me apart I don't like to fight.

I'm back with my love; I have no need to spite.

I have a feeling tonight will be a good night.

Amanda wants the details of the talk so I recite.

I promise I will try to be polite.

"My father hates the fact I'm now out of the closet.

Claims it's a sin because of the bible.

Doesn't understand I'm not doing it to be tribal.

It's not my choice to be gay!

Sometimes I wish I would just fucking fray!

I hate the fact that I'm trapped in gray.

I feel my homosexuality is a curse and I'm damned to suffer.

Then I turn to you and you become my buffer.

Being in your arms makes me warm inside.

Nothing will ever cause us to divide.

We are proud to be together and will take all the hate in stride."

"Maria you are strong and I admire you.

You're the love of my life, a fact I always knew.

My lips are meant to be pressed against yours.

Together we will kick down every single door.

We are a natural couple meant to be happy.

I'm not saying that just to be sappy.

Woman dating woman is frowned upon these days,

yet homosexuality has been around since man first raised."

"We are meant to be, I'm sorry I doubt.

I honestly just want to get up and shout!

My love for you is enduring and stout!

Now let's celebrate and spend a night out!"

Hanging out in Amanda's room near the end of freshman year,

she claims to own a bag that will make us cheer,

take us well into a new frontier.

I don't know if I should be excited or fear.

She tells me its weed she took from her brother,

and smelled it on the breath of her mother.

She bought a bowl for us to use,

along with a twenty-four pack of booze.

Nervous, I agree to let down my guard and get high.

Amanda lights up the bowl, she's defiantly not shy.

I take a hit, my very first I won't deny.

I pass the bowl back; Amanda takes another hit to comply.

After two bowls I feel happy and alive.

Now I'm beginning to feel deprived.

My heart aches for Amanda she needs to know

how I feel about her so a relationship can grow.

I can't take my eyes off her.

I know male is the sex I should prefer.

My heart has other plans.

Up and down her body I move my eyes to scan.

"What are you doing Maria why are you looking at me weird?"

I plant a kiss on her lips her confusion disappears.

"Maria I had no idea you liked me like that."

She smiles and winks that's the end of our chat.

The rest is history we have been together since.

She's my queen I have no need for a prince.

Sitting on Amanda's floor we are smoking away on a joint.

Life without weed wouldn't have a point.

I'm with my two loves all is right.

Amanda sure does look good in white.

I lean over and give her a passionate kiss.

Her tongue pressed against mine makes me melt away in bliss.

I smile at her and say, "let's go for a ride."

We jump in her car, cruise the town completely fried.

I stare out the window watching lights fly by.

The end of the world could damn near be nigh.

I wouldn't care, with my love I would die.

The moon is orange tonight it glows in the sky.

I unfasten my seat belt and roll down the window.

Stick my head out; allow my hair to blow in the wind.

Out of the corner of my eye I spot a hind.

Night time nature always seems so kind.

I look at Amanda give her a wink.

She makes a face that reminds me of a mink.

I blow her a kiss, her face goes pink.

I think it's time we had a few drinks.

I turn my head to look out the front widow.

All of a sudden our lives are in limbo.

Headlights of a car are heading straight at us.

Fear overcomes me as I cuss.

I reach for the wheel but it's too late.

How cruel that this is my fate?

(Tires squeal)

(Glass breaks)

(Metal bangs together)

My lifeless body lies motionless on the road.

Blood pours out of my ears as my body corrodes.

I'm standing over my own dead body.

From this side I really did dress too gaudy.

Amanda is unconscious in the car but is still alive.

It's my fault I didn't survive.

Amanda will blame herself; I hope she doesn't lose her drive.

I notice a shadow moving towards me,

should I stay or should I flee?

Wait…Damien?

(In a deep menacing voice)

No…

Two in the morning I'm asleep resting peacefully in bed,

an enjoyable dream occupies my head.

The phone rings I bolt awake from a deep sleep.

Quickly gather myself since I was just counting sheep.

I look at the caller I.D. my heart instantly drops.

I answer the phone fearing the worst.

Am I really this cursed?

"Mr. Staves this is Dr. Banks.

There is no easy way to say this so I'm going to be frank.

Your daughter was in a car accident.

We need you to come down to the hospital quick.

When you get here ask for Dr. Nick."

I wake up Tina and jump in the car.

Racing to the hospital again feels so bizarre.

Standing over my daughter's body overcome with tears,

my emotions are out of control the worst of my fears.

God blessed me with two wonderful children now they've been taken
away.

I want to go drown myself in the bay.

I'm lost; God's plan has never been this muddy.

I punch a wall out of anger, my hand becomes bloody.

I look to my wife for strength, she looks so lost.

I sense her soul has been covered in frost.

She moves towards me and hugs me tight.

We've descended into darkness, what happened to the light?

Losing a child is every parent's worst nightmare, not just mine.

Now that I've lost both, how will I ever be fine?

My foundation has been attacked and has become entwined

with doubt and gray since I no longer shine.

Tina holds me tight tries to provide me comfort.

"Everything will be fine we will pull through together.

We will go together and talk to Heather.

She will help us pull through and regain our strength.

I won't give up the fight; I will go through any length

to ensure we remain close and strong.

We will pull through even though the process will be long."

"You are my rock Tina, your strength I admire.

You have always been the one to inspire

me to grow strong in faith but I will not lie,

my faith is being challenged and might just die.

I will continue to preach, the Devil must not win.

I have to suck it up and grin.

With you by my side I will win the war

being fought against me, even if I must knock over every single door.

Losing my kids has destroyed me down to my core,

but the Devil defeating me will not go down in lore."

Tina kisses me as we say our goodbyes.

Another funeral is around the corner, much to my despise.

Everything I have ever had is now gone.

Taken far too early from me was my beloved swan.

The tears have not stopped falling from my eyes.

The pain of never having the chance to say goodbye

is unbearable, I swear I've lost the will to live.

You were my battery, gave me the ability to strive.

With you by my side I was beginning to thrive.

Now you're gone and I only have myself to blame.

Killing the one I love is my claim to fame.

I was behind the wheel; your life was in my hands.

We were out for a night of fun but life had other plans.

Because of me you are now dead.

I would have to put a bullet in my head

to ever forgive myself for killing the one I love.

Everyone can comfort me by saying you were taken by the one up above.

It's all a lie, your life was taken by me.

I want to hang up a noose from a tree.

Then my soul will be able to run free

and join up with yours on the other side.

Your death is only a temporary divide.

One day soon I will indeed be your bride.

I long for the day I die.

My life is now on a downhill slide.

I'm now completely void of pride.

So long my love.

One day soon I will again be your dove.

Sitting at the table in my home office needing time to be alone,

losing both of my children has left me frayed and prone,

to giving into temptation because I'm falling like a stone.

I pray for strength but I'm starting to feel disowned.

Pictures of my kids sit on the table in front of me.

They drove my life, they were the key.

I was suppose to die long before them

but they were taken before me, what did I do to deserve to be condemned?

I came down hard on Maria for coming out as gay.

It was the last thing I said to her she must have felt so betrayed.

If her own father didn't support her who would?

Of all people I should!

But now it's too late.

She goes to the grave with my disapproval on her plate.

I hope Jesus himself meets her at the gate.

Tells her I do love her and think she's great.

I should have been supportive of her decision.

Maybe then she wouldn't have been in that collision

and would still be around to carry out her vision

of being with Amanda while being successful and strong.

She's gone because I was in the wrong.

I hate myself I drove her out of the house that night.

Until the day I die I swear I will spite!

I'm beginning to sweat, I need to relax.

I know what I need in matter of fact.

I go up to Maria's room and enter inside.

The feeling is eerie, being in the room of a child who has died.

I take the feeling in for a moment, then being to cry.

She was a great daughter who never needed my guide.

I take out her bag of weed she has hidden under her bed.

I shouldn't do this but inside I'm dead.

I fill her bowl and light it up.

Smoke the bowl now I'm feeling good.

My mind is now a mess I feel even worse.

Weed is not a friend but a curse!

I hate myself and want to die!

I hate the fact that all I do is cry!

How can anyone think I'm special I'm nothing but a loser!

I bet people are nice to me because they feel bad.

They realize I'm pathetic and a deadbeat dad,

and are nice to me so I won't go mad.

I bet they would love to know that I'm on the verge

of insanity, so their perfect little world and mine is about to converge.

I would bet money my wife regrets mating with me,

She probably laughs at me in bed, ask her she will agree.

Negativity consumes my mind but what I say is true.

I'm a pathetic loser who's better off turning blue.

No one would care if I ended my life right now.

Maybe it's time to take one last bow.

Working in the kitchen I turn the radio on.

Navigate through the stations all the good ones are gone.

The radio plays nothing good, underground is where real music lives.

The radio use to be good what gives?

I'm cooking a nice dinner trying to take my mind off Maria.

It's not working, at the time it seemed like a good idea.

I hope this dinner will cheer up Steve.

Show him there still is good in the world and help him believe that he can move on from this tragedy and achieve

great things he can't image now because he's naïve.

The phone rings I pick it up and answer.

I don't recognize the number, I wonder who it is but why does it matter?

It's a potential client; he questions me like I'm taking a quiz.

I assure him I'm the right person for the job; I'm available to be his.

I need a new client to help myself get back on my feet.

The departure of my children has left me feeling incomplete.

Hopefully now I can get back on my seat.

Move forward in life down an empty street.

<u>Act III – Murdered Love</u>

Sitting in front of the graves, my breathing is heavy with rage,

the animal inside me is rattling its cage.

I'm soaked from the rain, drenched down to my core,

realizing the truth, Jesus did marry a whore!

How else could I have been left in this state of deplore?

My entire life I was lied to!

I stuck to those lies like glue.

One mistake that cost me my family!

How can God be so cruel?

My entire life I was a fool,

never again will I be a tool.

The sun doesn't shine through the window today,

maybe a sign I was lead astray?

My arms dangle next to me like they are made of clay.

My mind races lost in gray.

There are two empty seats up front

that no one will dare to confront

since they fear them like a couple of lit blunts.

My wife sits alone,

the front of the church will always be her zone.

She's beautiful and strong,

smiles at me like nothing is wrong.

I'm glad to be back,

even though my life has been tarnished in black.

I'm back again where I belong.

I take my place in front of the church.

My heart hurts as I fight back tears.

Lately I've fallen in love with beer.

It helps to numb the effects of this long, dark year.

Maybe I picked the wrong career.

Maybe I need to explore a new frontier.

Time to focus and begin the service.

Does my mind dancing around make you nervous?

It's hard to focus at times

but lack of concentration is no crime.

Good morning

(good morning).

An older gentleman lies tucked away in his bed.

Cancer has overtaken his body; his eyes are stricken with dread.

His body is weak, he begs for death to come.

After a long life he feels he's been reduced to a crumb.

His daughter is by his side holding his hand tight.

She should be overcome with fright

since her father is losing the fight,

but she smiles sensing he's nearing the light.

I enter the bedroom it feels depressed and cold.

The daughter greets me, she seems brave and bold.

Thanks me for helping her father in his time of need.

Tells me I'm doing a very good deed.

I greet the old man as a smile spreads across his face.

I can tell he's ready to move on to a better place.

He asks me, "How long have you been helping people die?"

I grab his hand and look him in the eye.

"Twenty-one years I've been ending people's pain.

Never once have I thought to abstain.

Even though helping you die is taboo in some people's heads,

there is no need to suffer when you're already dead."

"Do you only help people who are already damned to die?

Or are there others who ask for your help, to which comply?"

"I only help people who are terminally ill.

Helping anyone else would be an abuse of my skill."

The old man smiles, says he ready to go.

Kisses his daughter goodbye says he's proud to have watched her grow.

She holds his hand tight, tells him she knows.

I stick the needle into a vein in his arm.

Inject the poison into his body, he's not alarmed.

He smiles one last time as his eyes close for the final time.

His body might have died, but for eternity, survive will these rhymes.

Eating breakfast at the kitchen table, I have the home to myself.

Steve's back to work at the church, it's where he needs to be.

He's been lost, adrift alone in the sea.

I hope getting back to his routine will bring him glee.

There's a knock at the front door.

In my mind I slowly count to four.

Get up from the chair thinking I really need to go to the store.

Walk towards the door like answering it is a chore.

I open the door, shock fills my soul.

It's Amanda. with a look on her face that screams finding me was her goal.

She tells me we need to have a talk,

and not to look at her like she's a gawk.

We sit down at the kitchen table.

I look into her eyes, they seem unstable.

The past four months have taken its toll on her.

I can tell her death is the one she preferred.

"How can I help you Amanda?

You must have come to me for a reason."

"I know what you do Mrs. Staves…

you help people find their graves.

You help them die when they have given up hope.

You must be on some serious dope

to be at peace with the job you do.

How does it feel to turn people blue?"

"I help people die who are already dead,

who have a terminal illness and live in dread.

They suffer every day for no reason.

I'm helping people find peace, but it's viewed as treason.

Often viewed as murder, it's closer to putting an animal to sleep,

ending their torment so they no longer weep.

"I want you to help me die!

I'm void of life and long to fry.

Losing Maria was the death of me!

I know from my problems I shouldn't flee,

but I'm a zombie going through life mindlessly dead.

My soul has been destroyed along with my head.

Help me end this pain and reunite with my love.

I promise to have your back from up above."

"I can't help you Amanda, allow me tell you why.

I promise you I won't be shy.

I only help those who are terminally ill.

I don't help people die for the thrill.

I help them end the pain they are in.

When they die they leave with a grin.

You're heartbroken Maria is gone.

You will be fine come dawn.

We are all beat up over her death.

Do yourself a favor and catch your breath.

It's time for you to move on with your life."

"Mrs. Staves, I know how much Maria suffered.

I saw the scars on her chest from where she cut

due to the pain of having her choice of a lover viewed as smut.

She suffered from depression as I do now,

but contained strength greater than what I am allowed.

Her death is squarely on my hands.

That is knowledge I can't bear to stand.

I'm truly dead inside and want your help.

I'm in front of you beginning to whelp.

"I can't help you Amanda, get a hold of yourself!

You see the picture of Maria over on that shelf?

It's all I have left of my little girl.

My emotions inside me are caught up in a swirl.

I hurt just like you,

but I don't view my life as being through.

It's time for you to leave now.

Helping you die is something I simply won't allow.

I'm willing to talk to you and help you see

your life will continue and Maria is now free

from the suffering she endured and the pain she felt.

I know you hate the hand you've been dealt,

but be strong, you will survive and thrive

and turn around from your head first dive.

"I will leave you alone now Mrs. Staves but I will be back.

My heart and soul have turned pitch black.

We will talk again soon.

You will help me like you helped your mother-in-law June."

Pale and lifeless June Staves lies weak in her bed.

Cancer has destroyed her body, left her filled with dread.

Steve's eyes are red and filled with tears.

He's about to lose his mother, a fact that's now clear.

He holds her right hand tight and smiles at her.

a warm smile spreads across June's face, she moves her lips and slurs,

"I love you son, I'm glad you are here.

Even though my soul is about to disappear,

I will always be with you, smiling at you from above."

"I love you too mom, Tina will take good care of you.

For so long you have been my glue.

I'm honored to be here with you, to witness you depart.

I will miss you every second you are gone with all my heart.

But one day I will see you again

and we will be together in paradise, free from pain."

Tina enters the room, places her right hand on June.

Tells her she's about to enter a place far beyond the planets and moons,

where she will no longer suffer but be at peace.

Take a deep breath the life you know is about to cease.

June blinks, smiles and grips Steve's hand tight.

Whispers she's about to head toward the light.

Tina sticks a needle into her arm.

June's facial features remain calm, show no signs of alarm.

Her eyes close as she leaves the world behind.

A new angel has just been primed.

With an apple in hand I'm sitting at the kitchen table.

Steve's upstairs in the shower I fear he's becoming unstable.

I'm trying to remain strong since weak is not my label.

The loss of my children often seems like a fable

that ends with me hanging up a noose made of cable.

I often wish I could be a writer so I could create a book

that lets out the emotions that hide under the way I look.

I may seem strong but I never smile.

Inside the pain rips me apart and turns me hostile.

I take deep breaths to numb the pain, but the damage continues to compile.

I look to Steve for strength, but he's also lost in the dark.

I'm alone in the ocean as the only shark.

I will pull through I have enough strength,

even though I will have to battle at length.

There's a knock at the door I sense who it is.

I don't want to answer; I would rather take a quiz.

I get up from the table knowing my strength will be tested.

Being reminded of my daughter's death is worse than being molested.

I reach the front door and place my hand on the knob.

Just this once I wish I could be a snob.

ignore the knocking until it fades,

but it's my sworn duty to aid.

When people are down and need to talk

they put their faith in me to be their block.

I open the door and stare into Amanda's eyes,

they're bright red, she's obviously high.

I continue to stare and to my surprise,

I discover a determination not to compromise.

"I'm ready to die Mrs. Staves I need your help.

I'm not going to beg or yelp.

I bought a gun; it tastes so good in my mouth.

If I pull the trigger I will end up south.

You must pull the trigger I want to go north.

I promise you today is my last day on earth."

"Stop acting like Maria's death only affects you!

Try looking at it from my point of view!

I lost both of my children, not just one, two!

I will no longer be able to watch them grow!

I beg to have the days back when they were young and played in the snow.

I'm hurting and angry that they are gone!

I pop pills beginning at dawn

to numb the pain of losing my babies.

There are days I feel like I have rabies

and foam at the mouth for death to come!

But it doesn't, so I continue to feel like scum."

"The pain you feel, I feel too.

It completely consumes me, a fact I wish wasn't true.

I can no longer function, I'm completely crippled inside.

I know you don't want me here but our paths must collide.

I have an incurable disease, a fact that can't be denied.

You're a strong person full of pride.

Your husband looks to you as his guide.

You guys still have each other to be your rocks.

I'm alone, trapped in a box.

Help me end my life.

All I want is to be with my wife."

"Bitch how dare you think we feel the same!

I'm tired of playing your fucking game!

You don't have a son, who went fuckin' mad,

committed gruesome murders and felt glad!

Set his girlfriend on fire and blamed his acts on his father!

I don't understand why you bother

to come to me for help in my time of need!

My wounds are still fresh and continue to bleed!

Not only did I lose my Damien, I lost my Maria.

How that is part of God's plan, I have no fucking idea!

I buried both of my children when they should have buried me!

My loss is greater than yours, don't you agree?"

I open my mouth to speak but stop.

Mr. Staves is standing at the bottom of the stairs looking like slop.

Alcohol is strong on his breath; I smell it five feet away.

I can tell he's having a very rough day.

"Mr. Staves I'm sorry for your loss.

Maria was my world like yours…is the cross?

I'm here asking your wife for help so I can be with Maria again.

She's been my love since I was ten."

"Amanda it's time for you to leave.

Please leave us alone so we can grieve."

"Mr. Staves I just want…"

"You want to die I know."

"You see this? It's my gun.

I want your wife to pull the trigger and then she's done."

"Get out of my house Amanda and never return!

I'm not asking I'm being stern!

I lost my children, you lost a crush!

Don't say another word just go hush!

Turn around and walk out the door

keeping in mind you're a person I will never adore!"

"Mrs. Staves…"

"It's time for you to leave now Amanda!"

Mrs. Staves puts her arm around me and leads me to the door.

Whispers in my ear I'm a no good dirty whore.

As she opens the door I slap her across the face.

She spits in my face like I'm a disgrace.

Amanda slaps me for a second time I've had enough.

It's time for me to stand tough.

I push her with all my might; she falls to the ground.

The animal inside me has been found.

Amanda gets up, charges at me hard.

I lift her up; carry her across the yard,

slam her down on the road.

Deliver a kick to her ribs as my anger explodes.

Amanda gets up and retreats to the other side of the road,

then reaches for her gun that she no longer owns,

since it fell on the sidewalk and is now in Steve's hand.

Looks like I just ruined her perfect little plan.

Defeated, Amanda turns around to leave.

Drops her head and begins to grieve.

She didn't get the death she wished to achieve.

I begin to turn to look at Steve.

Out of the corner of my eye I notice a car

speed around a nearby curve with the driver smoking a cigar.

I have no time to react.

Yet another life is about to be subtract.

I'm hit at forty-five all goes black.

Standing over my body I can't believe I just died.

My death was gruesome I will not lie.

My skull was crushed by the car's front and back driver side tires.

It was a quick, painless way to retire.

I notice Amanda in a state of shock.

Overcome with tears she can't even talk.

She pulls out a knife she has hidden in her pocket.

Slits both her wrists then lies on the sidewalk to die.

I guess she won't be with Maria in the sky.

Steve is in a state of shock

kneels down by my body, gone is his rock.

I fear what is to become of him.

His future sure seems dim.

He screams out no and begins to cry.

I kiss him on the head to say goodbye.

Take a long look into his eyes.

I don't recognize this man.

Amanda soon appears next to me.

Her soul has finally been set free.

Out of the corner of my eye I notice a shadow.

More shadows appear, soon we are surrounded.

A man appears in front of me.

Damien? How can that be?

(in deep menacing voice)

No…

Kneeling beside the body of my love,

I'm beginning to doubt there's a God up above.

My entire family is now gone I seethe.

Why am I the only one left to breathe?

My body and soul is filling with hate

I'm shaking uncontrollably, stress is getting to me, it's now too late.

Amanda watched my wife die,

took it as a sign to kill herself and complied.

My foundation has been fractured multiple times over.

It's too late for me to ever find closure.

My first love has now become jaded.

I no longer feel human, I've been degraded!

The light that shined on me has faded.

Faith now lost, I can't be persuaded!

Swallowed whole in darkness seems to be recurring,

progressing in severity as though a cascade of genetic damage is occurring.

The beast locked inside me is stirring.

My fortress has been leveled to ashes I'm not slurring!

I look up to the stars,

it reminds me that I'm scarred.

Total Eclipse Of The Sun

I look into a mirror,

as my day of reckoning draws near.

Clears out my mind, allows it to freely float.

I'm not one to usually gloat,

and I don't want my words to be misquote,

but I want to grab you around the throat,

choke you out so you no never sing another note!

I'm losing my mind!

How could I have been so blind!?

To believe the lies of mankind!

I've lost everything I've ever had.

Tell me why the fuck I shouldn't be mad!

I burn with rage like the people of Riyadh.

I don't see that as being so bad.

Sitting on my recliner sipping on coffee,

thinking about my upcoming date that will surely be saucy.

Newly single and exploiting my goods,

maybe I'll take my man deep into the woods.

Recreate a time when I was young,

when the boys weren't nearly as hung.

My door slams (Bang!) as Steve walks in.

I jump from my chair nearly spilling the coffee on my skin.

I almost forgot he was coming in to talk.

The way he slammed the door was definitely a shock.

I look up at the clock,

then go to make a joke, but decide I don't dare mock.

Steve is different I can tell by his eyes.

This may be a session I have to improvise.

Steve sits down across from me.

Looks like a man capable of murder in the first degree.

I feel uneasy with Steve in the room.

He looks like a man being consumed

by the demons from below whom he allowed to enter.

The Steve I know is gone, no longer front and center.

I ask Steve how he's doing.

Inside I'm secretly stewing.

He stares at me, his eyes burning with fire.

Total Eclipse Of The Sun

The situation he's in is not one I admire.

"You want to know how I'm doing Heather?

You sure you don't want to discuss the weather?"

"I want to help you Steve, I need you to talk.

You have all the time you need; you're not on the clock."

"I quit my job; I'm no longer a pastor.

My life has turned into a complete disaster.

My son went mad and blamed it on me.

Then my daughter died, a fate unfair, don't you agree?

Thought life couldn't become any worse,

but it did because I'm fucking cursed!

I watched my wife die in the middle of the road!

This caused my soul to completely implode!

I dedicated my life to God and this is what I get?

Forsaken by God and asked to forget

the family I helped to create!

That was on its way to becoming great!"

"I know it hurts but you must move on

and accept the fact that your family is gone.

You're allowing anger to consume your soul,

and allowing hatred to take control.

God is giving you a test

because he knows you're strong and can handle the stress.

Let go of the negative and focus on the good.

Never feel like you're misunderstood.

I'm here to help, I understand your pain.

Believe me, one day God will end the rain

and allow the sun to shine on you again."

"God's not real, we are all that exists.

If he was, he wouldn't allow you to slit your wrists.

The hell I'm in seems unreal.

Feeling like this has no appeal.

A loving God would never allow such a thing.

Once you hit rock bottom, you never recover from the sting."

"You're suffering from depression and need help."

"I'm consumed with anger not sub coming to sorrow,

even though I wish there would be no tomorrow."

"You're severely depressed; it's not a death sentence.

Try to remember you're still God's apprentice.

You're a good man, don't let that trait go.

Tina would never want you to be so low.

Cheer up and go do something fun.

The past can never be undone."

Steve shakes his head then gets up to leave

he will pull through, he must believe.

Act IV – A War No One Can Win

Sitting Indian style on top of a grass covered hill,

overlooking the bustling city below is such a thrill.

The sun shines bright overhead today.

The synagogue is filled with people who pray.

The sidewalks are filled with people who smile.

People filled with joy is more my style.

Red, yellow, green the lights turn,

keeping the traffic in control so no one gets burned.

Skyscrapers stretch far into the sky.

I enjoy standing on their very tops because being so high

allows me to feel like God,

overlooking my domain realizing it's flawed.

Yet I can't help but applaud.

I've built my empire from the ground up.

Time to kick back and sip from my cup.

The sun shines bright on me it feels so warm,

but the sun shining bright is not out of the norm.

Rabbits play around me, they come in swarms.

They are quickly learning I'm the creator, so they begin to conform.

The last thing I want to do is misinform.

Beautiful flowers cover my hill top.

I love to pick them, it's addicting, I just can't stop.

Bring them up to my nostrils to take in their smell.

They smell more like Heaven rather than Hell.

The sky is blue, not a cloud in sight,

yet I can't shake the feeling that something is not right.

I've become overcome with fright.

I scan the land sensing danger,

then I'm approached by a stranger.

Gives me an ominous warning to fear the sky,

leaves me with a simple goodbye.

I look up towards the sky,

what I see causes me to cry.

A bomb is falling, heading straight for my city.

The end result will not be pretty.

I take shelter on the hill.

The bomb hits destroying my will.

A mushroom cloud forms high in the sky.

I blink several times fighting not to close my eyes.

Sorrow invades my soul.

I know my city has been reduced to coal

but I'm afraid to look,

since there will be no happy ending in this book.

Walking down the broken roads of the town

brings tears to my eyes that causes me to frown.

Smoke fills the air coming from the burned ashes of homes.

People's yards are filled with the shattered remains of their gnomes.

Dust and twisted steel occupy the spots once held by my skyscrapers.

Dust blows around in the air, along with the tattered remains of paper.

The smell of rotting corpses invades my nostrils.

A smell I will never forget until I'm a fossil.

Bodies of my people line the broken roads.

It's just a matter of time until their bodies corrode.

Most bodies are unrecognizable, vaporized by the heat.

An image so gruesome, from my mind I wish to delete.

Walking down the broken roads further into town,

I stumble upon a mask of a clown.

It was used on Halloween by a resident named Jake.

I pick it up for keeps even if it's for nostalgic sake.

At the heart of downtown I enter a park.

Once lively and bright it has now become dark.

The clouds above me open up and unleash their water.

I feel like a pig being lead to slaughter.

I fall to my knees and begin to cry.

Why must my demise be nigh?

Anger consumes my heart.

I no longer feel so smart.

My arms dangle next to me numb.

This is what it's like to feel like scum.

I let out a scream in rage!

I've entered a brand new age!

My mind's chaotic, can't focus on a goddamn thing.

Right now would be a perfect time to sing.

Help to take away some of the sting

of no longer being the king

of my once great empire.

Now I'm lost burning in fire.

Total Eclipse Of The Sun

I compose myself look towards a single remaining tree.

A shadow of a man stands next to it with no intent to flee.

His eyes are red and burn right through me.

Mouths the words, "I'm now free."

He holds a key and an open lock.

Smiles at me, he's beginning to mock.

Points towards a noose hanging from the tree.

A banshee appears next to me, I have no chance to plea.

I walk to the tree place the noose around my neck.

Close my eyes tight; think back to the time I was in Quebec.

I crawl out of bed before my alarm goes off.

Put my hand over my mouth as I begin to cough.

My throat is dry I could use a drink.

Not a drink you just get from the sink.

My body is warm and my head covered in sweat.

The shirt I fell asleep in is soakin' wet.

A result of another long restless night,

a theme that is quickly becoming trite.

Total Eclipse Of The Sun

The robes I used to preach still hang in my closet.

Wearing them allowed me to feel like a prophet.

But God is dead to me, I resigned three weeks ago.

Following the death of my love I lost control.

What kind of God leaves you all alone?

Throws you blindly into the unknown?

My heat is filled with anger, soul with rage

I've entered a brand new age.

I'm losing my mind more everyday.

I swear I hear Satan calling me to come out and play.

I go to the kitchen grab myself a beer.

Sit down at the table and begin to jeer

at the picture of Damien still hanging on the wall.

Looking at it makes me want to get into a brawl.

I can't stand it anymore it needs to go!

He began my downfall you know?

I pull out a lighter set fire to the picture.

Accidently burn my finger, damn a blister.

I drop the picture to the floor, watch it burn to ash.

Total Eclipse Of The Sun

No longer will he and I have to clash.

I'm a shell of my former self, I feel like I'm dead.

I hate the fact there is chaos in my head.

I need a fix to get me through the day,

then sit down and read a story that's risqué,

since I'm a man and have urges to obey.

I pull out my bag of weed laced with ecstasy.

Smoking this shit is my worst enemy.

It puts me in a state of suicidal tendency,

but thriving in the dark is my specialty.

What kind of place am I in mentally?

I crash on the couch and light up a bowl.

Soon I will no longer be in control.

One bowl down, I load up another.

Marijuana has become my new lover.

Three bowls deep, I'm struggling to move.

My body feels great yet for so long I have disapproved.

My eyes are red and I'm smiling for no reason.

I couldn't even tell you the current season.

I turn my head to the right.

I'm suddenly overcome with fright.

I'm taken back by what I see.

Sitting next to me…is another me.

He smiles at me and gives me a wink.

For the next minute I rapidly blink.

He doesn't vanish, what I'm seeing is real.

He speaks, "here is the deal,

I'm that voice inside you urging you to steal.

I'm the monster you want to be.

But you lack the courage, don't you agree?

I've been trapped inside you for so long.

Keeping me inside was wrong.

Now I'm out and here to claim my place

as the real Steve who lacks grace."

In a state of shock I don't know what to say.

That whole speech has me blown away.

The man takes out a gun and points it at me.

I look around but have nowhere to flee.

He pulls the trigger and I hear a bang.

Why must I feel like I'm in Pyongyang?

I turn and cover my head.

For some reason I'm not dead.

I turn back around.

The man is nowhere to be found.

Rattled, I go to the kitchen and begin to drink.

I drink so much I throw up in the sink.

Stumble up stairs to my bed.

I want to keep drinking but black out instead.

Wake up the next morning with my head killing me.

It happens every morning now that I'm a retiree.

I go to the kitchen to make coffee.

I have a bad addiction to caffeine.

I go to fire up the coffee machine, it doesn't work.

An inconvenience that leaves me a little irked.

I throw the machine to the ground and watch it shatter.

The noise awakens my mind, begins the chatter.

With coffee not an option I take out the Jaeger.

Down a fifth that hits me like a dagger.

I go up to the bedroom and put some clothes on.

Kiss the picture next to my bed of my now departed swan.

Return downstairs and go to the back door.

Open the door now I'm off to explore.

I enter a forest not too far from my house, begin a three minute walk.

Above my head flies a hawk.

It's on the hunt for food.

The hawk is putting me in an evil mood.

I exit the forest and enter a field once inherited by slaves.

I conclude my walk by arriving at four graves.

I kneel down before them and feel my will to live begin to cave.

These are the graves of my family including my mother.

There's still room for the grave of another.

Set aside for me when it's my time to die

that deep down inside I feel coming so standby.

Kneeling before Tina's grave I can't help but cry.

As rage boils in my eyes…

The rock I leaned on was taken from me.

It makes me want to drown myself in the sea!

I devoted my life to God.

Lead my heard of sheep and won their applaud.

But now my eyes are open,

with my spirit completely broken,

by a so called loving God.

I can't believe I fell for that fraud!

My daughter was taken as well.

I was left behind to dwell in this hell.

She had her whole life in front of her,

that now will never occur.

How fair is that?

Take my family and leave me to combat

the war raged against me on my own…

…a war no one can win I grown.

Standing in front of Damien's grave…

…he disowned me and all that I gave.

I admit I now understand,

winning the war was never part of the plan.

Damien went completely mad.

Lost the rule of man in his head and was glad.

He will be pleased to know his very own dad

is losing his mind and turning bad.

I hate the little fuck!

Then again that's my luck.

Get blamed for his actions,

even though I gave him a positive reaction.

It killed me and I began to fracture.

Felt like I was left behind after the rapture.

I'm done with him!

He got me to stop singing my hymns.

Just like he predicted…I would sink not swim,

and fall victim to my life turning grim.

I'm pissed off and beginning to spite.

I kick over Damien's head stone…I don't want it in my sight!

Total Eclipse Of The Sun

I look back towards the forest wanting to continue to explore,

since standing in one place can become a bore.

I look ahead since off in the horizon is a road.

I notice a car beginning to slow.

People have problems minding their own business.

Unfortunately for them I'm not afraid to burn bridges.

I turn around and head back into the forest.

The chatter in my mind is beginning to sound like a chorus.

I head west along an old dirt trail

that was once praised as a holy grail.

It's now hard to spot being overgrown with plants

and infested with dirt hills occupied by ants.

There's a slight breeze blowing among the leaves.

I hear footsteps behind me, an animal I perceive.

The footsteps continue I turn to take a look.

Nothing is there, were you expecting a hook?

Turn back around and get quite a scare

that causes my arm hair to stick straight up in the air.

A shadow walks across the trail up ahead.

Walks like a human, I begin to dread.

I slowly make my way up to where it crossed.

The forest is a place I would hate to get lost.

I take a look around and off in the distance

I notice red eyes staring at me confirming the shadow exists.

I pick up the pace and continue to move forward.

If I stay on the trail I can't get cornered.

Up ahead I see a river,

along with a dam built by a beaver.

I reach the river and stand at the edge.

I smile remembering my pledge

to live my life completely devoted God.

You're no longer the one I laud!

Staring at my reflection in the water, there's a tap on my back.

I turn and face a young boy dressed in black.

"What are you doing out here mister?

Are you some kind of drifter?"

"I decided to go for a walk son,

that honestly hasn't been too much fun.

What are you doing out here all alone?

This is not a very safe zone."

"I'm out here with my parents; we are staying at our cabin.

I got bored and decided to go for a walk before the sky begins to blacken."

"You shouldn't wonder off kid.

I bet your parents are pissed off that you did."

"My cabin is just over there.

Besides they are too intoxicated to care."

I look towards the horizon…

…sure enough there's a cabin.

"What are you doing out here mister?

Your presence here isn't exactly a fixture."

"I came out here to die son.

Doesn't that sound like fun?"

"Why are you going to die?

Doesn't your family want to say goodbye?"

"My family has been taken from me.

Not just my wife, or my son, or my daughter, all three.

I've lost the will to carry on.

With the sun now setting, I plan to be dead before dawn."

"I'm sorry you lost your family sir,

but negative events are bound to occur.

God has a plan for you.

Put your trust in him and he will pull you through

the darkness that's sticking to you like glue."

"God is a fake!

Time to open your eyes and become awake!

What kind of God takes a man's family?

Then throws him into darkness and agony?

If there is a God I hate him!

Best you hate him too before your future turns grim."

Total Eclipse Of The Sun

"I'm sorry you feel that way sir,

but believe me one day you will again be with her.

The wife you love, along with your kids.

It's not the end of the world that they died god forbid.

You will pull through, try to smile.

Being down and miserable is not your style."

The young boy stretches out his arms and gives me a hug.

He's playing with fire acting so smug.

I place my hand on his head; rub my fingers through his hair.

My eyes feel like they are on fire, I swear.

Take my other hand and run it down his face.

He miscalculated assuming I still contain grace.

I place my hands firmly on his head.

Snap his neck quick, he falls to the ground dead.

I drop to the ground, begin to sniff his body.

He smells like a Bobby.

I have a strong desire for blood.

Evil is flowing out of me in a flood.

I pick up his body and toss it in the river.

God was unable to save him, go figure.

I turn my attention to the cabin.

I wonder if the boy's mother is wearing satin.

The sun is nearly set.

The dark of the night I must offset.

Time to build a fire.

For the night I will retire.

Sitting around the fire that is now going strong,

the night has set in I have a feeling it's going to be long.

I pull out a bag of weed and load up a bowl.

Feeling like a million bucks all night long is my goal.

I take out a flame and put it to the bowl.

Inhale its content; absorb it all the way down to my soul.

Pack a second bowl since I enjoyed the first so much.

Inhale it slow to fully enjoy its soothing touch.

I fall backwards and lay on the ground.

I close my eyes feeling profound.

Drift off to sleep to the sound of an owl.

The sun will soon be up, and then the animal will begin its prowl.

My eyes shoot open to the sound of a cracking branch.

I jump to my feet; I should have remained on watch.

I notice red eyes staring at me from the shadows.

I begin to move, the red eyes follow.

I stop and ask who's there?

A voice speaks, "not a bear."

I demand the fiend to show himself.

A shadow of a man appears in the light of the fire.

He's wearing familiar attire.

The man takes the form of a real person.

It's Steve, the man I met in the house.

His appearance will surely cause a rouse.

He takes a seat next to me and begins to smile.

I'm expecting him to become hostile.

"Very good Steve I enjoyed the show.

I knew it wouldn't take much to get you to blow.

A few references to God and off you went.

You're a regular ole Harvey Dent.

Start out good and preaching what's right,

but as soon as day turns to night,

you lose your mind, it's such a delight!

It does help that I'm now calling the shots.

I've always been a powerful boss.

You would never listen to me!

Locked me up in a cage and threw away the key!

It feels so good to finally be free!

Free to cause chaos and havoc!

Unleashed has been a ruthless savage.

Enjoy the rest of the night Steve.

Tomorrow morning will be fun, you better believe."

I go to respond but Steve is gone.

Vanished in thin air, I guess it's off to dawn.

Dawn breaks as the sun begins to rise.

I've been up the rest of the night preparing for my demise.

The couple in the cabin is in for a real surprise.

I hope both of them have been baptized.

Time for action, I'm tired of making implies.

I begin my walk towards the cabin.

My mind races imagining what's about to happen.

I move slowly through the forest not wanting to be heard.

I plan on catching them completely off guard.

I begin to hear footsteps all around me.

Multiple footsteps, how can that be?

Laughter begins to echo all around me.

Shut up, I'm trying to get there undetected don't you see!?

The laughter continues so I stop.

Quickly to the ground I drop.

Scan the land around me to see who's there.

I sense evil in the air.

I notice shadows standing all around me,

so I close my eyes and count to three.

Get back up and pick up the pace for the cabin

refusing to look around because that's my habit.

I reach the cabin and let out a sigh of relief.

I'm beginning to feel like a thief.

I pick a window and go up to it.

I'm a little nervous I will admit.

Look through the window to find out what's inside.

Just what I was looking for, it's the groom and bride.

I light up a joint

stare through the window

my targets are sleeping

holding each other tight

like it's their last…

…and it is.

I light up a joint

continue to stare through the window

my targets are still sleeping

holding each other tight

like it's their last night together

trust me it is.

Empty beer cans litter the bedroom floor.

The wife looks like a stereotypical whore.

They became too intoxicated to know their son had wondered off.

When they find out he's dead, they will surely scoff.

I move on to the next window.

Peer inside to search for info.

Don't want any surprises when I enter the place.

Unexpected surprises can lead to an unfortunate fate.

I look through the window and scan the kitchen.

I see a picture of Jesus, they are definitely Christian.

I notice a sharp knife sitting on the table.

My targets getting a hold of that could be fatal.

I move on to another window and peek inside.

It's the living room and to my delight

there's nothing that could harm me.

Time to move to the front door, I hope I don't need a key.

I move to the front door place my hand on the knob.

Panic for a moment but I'm too far along to stop.

Turn the knob, the door swings open.

I smile and become filled with emotions.

The couple sound asleep are rudely awakened.

Their eyes open to the sound of laughter

from a god up above cursing out their world.

That god is me.

With a gun in hand I tie the woman to the bed.

Place the gun into the back of the man's head.

Instruct him to move to the living room.

He moves slowly sensing doom.

He begs me not to harm his son.

I tell him too late that deed has been done.

He tells me I'm a monster and will surely burn.

I tell him what happens to me is none of his concern.

He tells me to put the gun down and face him like a man.

I tell him that's not part of the plan.

I pull out the knife from the kitchen and place it against his throat.

Slit it quick, he drops to the floor; he has said his final note.

I return to the bedroom to take care of the wife.

I hope she has enjoyed her life.

I enter the room, there stands my son

motioning to me to finish what must be done.

I blink several times not believing my eyes.

All that's there is a tied up woman who cries.

She demands to know who I am.

I don't tell her, all she will do is condemn.

I pull out her tongue and slice it off.

Choking on blood she begins to cough.

I stick the knife into her back and severe her spine.

She's now just a head on a stick, with me that's fine.

I look deep into her eyes, she longs for death.

I allow her to take one final breath.

Place my gun in her mouth and pull the trigger.

Place my hand near my mouth and blow on my finger.

I turn around to exit the bedroom.

There stand's Steve, I'm overcome with a sense of doom.

He draws a gun and points it at my head.

Sticks it to the side of my head and tells me I'm dead.

I catch a glimpse of myself in a mirror.

I'm alone in the room holding the gun to my head.

I close my eyes overcome with dread.

(Gun shot rings out)

Act V – Chaos Venit Ordiem

"We have one that's still alive!"

"Let's get him out of here and begin our drive!

Make sure he's still alive when we arrive!"

"I'm Dr. Lewis what do we have?"

"Male, mid to late forties,

apparent self inflicted gunshot wound to the head.

We found two others with him who are dead.

The body of a child washed up along the shore of the Red.

The two others found dead with this guy are his parents.

We suspect he murdered all three."

"Thank you, we will do our best to make sure he survives."

I'm surrounded by darkness, I'm straining to see

see anything at all even if it's just a tree.

I'm surrounded by laughter echoing in the dark.

Total Eclipse Of The Sun

I reach for my lighter to make a spark

but I can't find it. In matter of fact

there is nothing around me I must truly be cracked.

All of a sudden I'm thrust up into blinding light.

Everything around me turns to white.

The light hurts my eyes it's far too bright!

I feel myself climbing but to what height?

I'm thrust through clouds and placed on a solid surface.

In front of me is the bottom of a staircase I'm feeling nervous.

I look towards the top of the stairs and see a gold gate.

I must have died and been put in a spiritual state.

That must be the gate to Heaven!

I saw it in a dream when I was seven.

But why am I here?

I caused three people to disappear

by ending their lives far too soon,

one fateful day before noon.

What have I done?

I was a harmless man not one to use a gun.

I feel a need to climb the steps.

I hope the top isn't a hex.

I climb the stairs and reach the top,

find a surprise that makes my heart want to pop.

Tina stands in front of the gate.

I give her a huge smile, seeing her again feels so great.

"Tina why am I here? I've done terrible things,

nothing worth of being treated like a king."

"Steve I'm here to explain a few things to you.

What I'm about to tell you is a lot to chew,

but it will stick with you like glue.

The good lord never turned his back on you.

Even after you turned your back on him and colored your soul black and
blue."

"I murdered a child along with his parents Tina."

"I'm well aware of the sins you committed Steve,

the last thing I am is naïve.

Our God is a very loving God,

he accepts us and all of our flaws.

He forgives you for killing those people,

just like he forgave me for playing god with a needle."

"I broke the commandment not to murder.

I'm not just some low life burglar."

"Steve…you…did not…kill those people.

The disease you had left you feeble."

"What are you saying Tina?"

"We are made in God's image Steve."

"Yes I know Tina."

"What do you think when you hear

we are made in his image?"

"He designed our bodies after him."

"You're wrong Steve our bodies are not made in his image.

Now I want you to really listen.

Our minds are created in his image.

Our minds are created to have no limits.

Our minds are powerful and when abused

they no longer help us to improve,

but turns on us and break.

The pain you experienced was never fake.

You fell into a severe depression that destroyed your mind.

As soon as Damien died you where never fine.

My death was the event that snapped your mind.

The good person you once were was left behind.

"What about the shadows and voices I experienced?"

"Those were a creation of your powerful mind.

Your mind broke loose and became unconfined.

You lost the ability to reason,

at that point you were defeated.

The other Steve you met was created by your mind.

In the vein of a split personality he was designed.

Every person contains an inherit evil inside of them,

locked away deep inside fighting to be unleashed.

Yours was unleashed when you lost your mind.

The good Steve disappeared and became blind.

The evil Steve your mind created became the real you.

I told you this was a lot to chew."

"I don't even know what to say Tina."

"The same thing happened to our son.

That's why we lost the son who was ready to stun,

inherited the one who was evil,

and whose actions were cynical.

He's here in Heaven with me.

Just like the way it was meant to be."

"What about our daughter?"

"She's here too don't you worry,

as is Amanda, Mia, your mother and your father."

"I have to ask, is Maria still gay?"

"Yes she is Steve, her and Amanda both

and Steve, I don't want to hear you loath."

"So homosexuality is not a choice?"

"No, homosexuality is not a choice.

Yet on earth they still don't have much of a voice.

In fact we are all born with a homosexual gene.

It comes out in some and in others, remains behind the scene.

"You have blown my mind Tina.

Even more so than the agility of a ballerina."

"You know all once in Heaven.

With this kind of knowledge you never need a weapon

to take away ones aggression,

and pull them out of their recession."

"So…am I going to be let in?

Since I no longer support an evil twin?"

"It's not your time to join us in Heaven."

"You mean I'm going back to earth?

Where my name has lost its worth?

I will spend the rest of my life in prison,

that's not a positive vision."

"God still has a plan for you on earth.

Consider this a brand new birth."

"What's his plan for me?"

"Whatever you make it out to be."

"Can I ask you one more question?

Along with a favor to apologize to God for all my transgressions?"

"Yes you can Steven,

and your favor has already reached completion."

"What's all in Heaven?"

"Everything your mind can imagine and then some.

One day sit down and chew on some gum.

Write out a list of everything you want in Heaven.

It will all be here, plus more that will leave you with an unforgettable impression."

"I expect to have a lot of free time to make that list.

It will be extensive since you insist. "

"Life on earth is quick you will be here soon.

Next time you will be greeted by your mother June."

"Can I see her before I return to earth?"

"No, but someone does want to see you before you leave.

Hold it together this will be hard for you to believe."

The gold gate to Heaven opens; I'm blinded by a light.

Yet I'm happy knowing everything will be alright.

The gate closes; I can't believe who stands in my sight.

Its Damien, no longer filled with spite.

He gives me a hug, apologizes for hurting me.

Seeing him again fills my heart with glee.

He informs me the entire family is here waiting for me,

and that patience is the key.

We will be together again.

Everything will be perfect then.

Damien tells me it's time for me to go.

I tell him I already know.

I drop to my knees in crippling pain.

A pain so intense my strength begins to drain.

My vision begins to narrow

until everything around me turns to black.

"How's the suspect doing?

Did he survive?"

"He was in very bad shape when he arrived.

Was technically dead for ten minutes,

but he must be a man who enjoys his spinach,

because his will to live is strong.

He's alive, and even though what he did was sick,

I'm proud we were able to save his life."

"When will he be able to answer for his crimes?

I don't want him free for an extended period of time."

"We can't put a time-table on his recovery.

We do expect it to take a couple of years for him to be able

to stand trial since his wound was fatal.

His brain was deprived of oxygen from being dead.

His wound was a severe one to the head.

He will need to relearn how to walk and talk.

It will be awhile before his trail is on the clock."

"Thank you doctor we will keep in touch."

Two years have passed since I shot myself in the head.

It's nice to be back sleeping in my own bed.

My recovery was long, but I accepted the challenge given to me by God.

I hope I made him proud and won his applaud.

My memories of the terrible events I'm responsible for are gone.

I feel blessed to be given a second dawn.

I remember my meeting with Tina very well.

I'm glad to know her departure is a temporary farewell.

I'm nervous facing the fate of being locked up in a cell.

But I will take this opportunity as a chance to excel.

I've been charged with my crimes and will face trial.

I will apologize for my actions and won't hide in denial.

Until then I'm out on bail,

blessed to not be rotting away in jail.

It's a beautiful Monday morning the sun is shining bright.

I stand by a window and take in the sight.

The grass is long and green,

the flowers across the street are a sight to be seen.

I move to the front door and step outside.

Take a deep breath and nearly begin to cry.

It feels so good to be alive; I will take what happens to me in stride.

I trust in the lord and will follow his guide.

Still standing in my yard I'm approached by an elderly lady.

Not an event that happens to me daily.

She tells me she has a bad feeling about some man

that is coming to carry out an evil plan,

and is worried about my neighbor Anne.

Not recognizing the lady I ask her how she knows Anne,

but answering my question isn't part of her plan.

She turns and walks away leaving with a smile.

I guess leaving people hanging is her style.

I turn my head to the right and notice a man walking my way.

He's wearing a hooded sweatshirt that's gray.

One of his hands is in the sweatshirt pocket.

I have a suspicion he's tripping on acid.

Anne is outside in her yard across the street.

It's a warm morning she's outside in her bare feet.

The man has his eyes squarely on her.

Something bad is about to occur.

I walk across the street and cut off the man.

Ask him what he's doing moving shadily towards Anne.

He tells me she's his ex and wants to talk.

Anne's taste in men is definitely a shock.

Anne tells the man to beat it she's done.

She no longer considers him her Hun.

I tell him you heard the lady now scram,

she's no longer falling for your scam.

He removes his hand from his pocket to reveal a gun,

tells me he's not here to have fun.

The bitch needs to die for being a tramp.

I tell him to move along, you're not a champ.

He puts the gun to my head and tells me to move.

I stare into his eyes having something to prove.

Tell Anne to go inside and lock the doors,

then tell the man she's no longer yours.

"You will turn around and never return,

or you will wish you were never born."

"You're cocky old man who's playing with fire,

step aside before you fate turns dire!"

"I'm not afraid to die young man,

that allows me to ruin your plan."

"Of course you're not afraid to die!

It doesn't take a fucking spy

to figure out who you are.

How are you not locked up behind bars?

You're the worst monster this town has ever seen!

That boy you killed wasn't even a teen!"

"You know of my past so why are you here?

Making your former lover disappear

makes you no better than me.

Not a difficult concept to understand, I'm not speaking in Cree."

"I've lost faith in the human race

since they showed a monster like you grace,

by setting you free on bail!

That was the final nail

driven deep into my heart!

I bet you feel so smart,

by tricking the legal system into letting you free!

I can't begin to imagine your glee!"

"I will pay for my actions by spending the rest of my days behind bars.

Walk away before you lose your freedom of seeing the stars."

"No Mr. Staves I'm here with a plan!

A plan that just expanded to make up for the grace of my fellow man.

Not only will I end the life of Anne,

I'm going to end yours and bury your ashes in the sand!"

"The police are on their way you better make it quick.

It's your move now slick."

(The sounds of sirens are heard coming from the horizon.)

"The bitch called the police I shouldn't have expected anything less.

The only thing she's good for is stress!

Time to move into your house,

no one's there since you lost your children and spouse."

With a gun held to the back of my head,

I'm forced down into my basement by Anne's ex Fred.

He commands me to sit on a chair,

then tells me to say a prayer.

He ties me up tight to the chair,

tells me I shouldn't have interfered in his affairs.

"You shouldn't have gotten in my way Steve!

Now I'm going to make you believe,

this is the worst ass beating you have ever received!"

"Do your worst to me Fred.

Just make sure I'm unable to move off a bed,

because if I get loose,

I won't stop beating you when you begin to bruise.

I will disfigure all your tattoos,

and then when you beg for mercy I will refuse."

Fred smiles and then punches me in the face.

Continues his assault at a rapid pace.

Left, right the blows keep coming.

Inside my ears I begin to hear a buzzing.

Fred stops his assault to shake his hand.

His last punch left his hand jammed.

I spit out blood as he shakes his hand in pain.

He might not know it but I think it's a sprain.

"What's wrong Fred did you hurt your hand?

My skull hurts a lot more than sand."

"You are in no position to talk!

Shut your mouth before I end your ability to walk!"

"Untie me Fred and fight me like a man!

Toss your gun in the trash can!

We fight fist to fist,

with no weapons to come to your assist!"

"You would like that wouldn't you Steve?

That's a goal you will never achieve.

I'm done with you Steve this ends now!

Your life continuing I will not allow!"

"So you're going to play god and decide my fate?

That's the job the prosecutor and judge have on their plates."

"They don't have the fortitude to put you to death!

I do because I'm high on meth,

and have no remorse for a monster like you.

Killing those innocent people will be the day you rue!"

"Do what you must Fred but you will be no better than I.

You will realize this when you're no longer high."

"I'm bringing justice to a murderer not killing innocent lives.

It's time to end this before the police arrive.

It's only a matter of time before they figure out we're down here.

My gun will be the last sound entering your ears."

Fred presses his gun against the side of my head.

His hand is shaky, swollen and red.

I close my eyes and wait for the shot.

Doing good was the goal I always sought.

At least I'm the one to die and not Anne.

I hope saving her is in fact God's plan.

I'm glad Fred decided to take this route.

Didn't shoot me on the spot, shoot Anne, then flout…

…all of a sudden a shot rings out.

I open my eyes Fred lies dead off to my side.

A bullet entered through the back of his head and came out his eye.

I hear a gun click, turn back to my left,

there stands a cop I'm beginning to feel blessed.

He walks up to me puts his gun against my head.

Turns out I had him completely misread.

"Nice to see you again Steven,

karma is now about to get even.

You're too dangerous to be kept alive.

Too damn bad you are about to commit suicide.

I tried to save you but you were already dead.

Ended Fred's life without a tear shed,

then put a bullet again into your head.

Once a monster always a monster,

now that monster has been conquered."

The officer pulls the trigger,

being shot in the head again feels bitter.

Standing in front of my dead body that's still tied to the chair,

the officer plants Fred's gun on me as he sneers.

Carefully moves my body and lies it on the ground.

Lays my body on its back to show off the entry wound.

My death has been staged as a suicide.

No one will care they wanted me crucified.

The officer picks up Fred's body sits it on the chair,

ties up the body to make that point clear.

I murdered him in cold blood.

People will believe it since my name has been dragged through the mud.

The officer now done with his deed returns upstairs.

One day karma will strike him down for his dark affair.

I follow him upstairs to see him out the door.

I walk towards the door but stop before I can count to four.

There's a man sitting in my recliner smiling at me.

He supports a pointed goatee.

He's smoking a cigar that's held in his right hand.

There's a snake wrapped around his left that listens to his commands.

He wears a top hat that looks brand new,

along with a suit and a pair of black shoes.

"Hello Steven it's nice to finally meet you.

I know my appearance can be considered taboo.

I usually have my minions do this for me

but, hear me out since you might agree.

You are too big of a challenge for them."

"Lucifer I take it?"

"Very good Steven I'm here to make a deal with you.

It's a great deal so hear me through.

I want you to be my right hand man.

I'm honestly your biggest fan.

Together we will rule planet earth.

That's how much I think you're worth.

You will have unlimited power over your domain.

That's the ultimate gift, leaves you with nothing to gain."

"I'm going to be with my family in Heaven.

My fate is not in question."

The front door opens, a bright light shines into the house.

Looks like it's time for me to head out.

Lucifer hates the light, fades back into the dark.

Looks like the Lord has silenced his bark.

I step into the light, the door closes behind me

as I rise up to Heaven to finally free.

I'm placed at the bottom of the staircase here I go again!

I run up the stairs full steam ahead.

I reach the top where I'm greeted by June.

Welcomes me to Heaven, tells me I have left my cocoon.

The gate of Heaven opens I step inside.

The rest of eternity begins now, a fact that's not implied.

Bio and Book Notes

Hello, I'm Tyler Zempel, author of Total Eclipse Of The Sun. I'm 25 years old and currently live in Macomb, Michigan. I'm from a small town called Rogers City, Michigan. I was born and raised there. I graduated from Rogers City High School in 2007. I graduated from Northwood University in 2011 with a Bachelor's degree in Business Management. I'm currently an Assistant Manager at Payless Shoe Source.

Writing has been a hobby of mine my entire life. I have always had a very creative mind. This book has been a long time coming. I put everything I had into creating it. I'm very proud of it and the way it has turned out. With that said, I wrote this book for me. Everything I have ever written, I wrote for myself. I am my hardest critic. I'm never satisfied with what I create, I always strive to become better and improve. For the first time I feel like I'm ready to publish something I wrote for the rest of the world to read.

I started writing this book in early 2012. The original concept was going to be a book about a man trying to survive in a post apocalyptic world and was going to have a very strong political theme to it. The book turned out completely different. The book is about a pastor, the ultimate good guy, and his fall into madness and redemption. The book is about depression and mental illness and the effects they have on people who suffer from those disorders. The book is a work of fiction. The people are made up and so are the events that take place. The emotion of the book is very real. As a person who once suffered from depression, I took my emotions and feelings from that time and put them into this book. I wrote this book as dark and as real as possible to fully capture the true feeling of depression.

I want to share this book with the world now it hopes of inspiring people who suffer from depression to continue moving forward in their battle with it by showing them there is light at the end of the tunnel. No matter how dark your life seems, there is always a light at the end. I'm living proof of that. Instead of harming myself or turning to suicide as the answer to my problem, I turned to writing. I took all of those negative thoughts and feelings and used them as good to create art. Along with a loving family (who mean more to me then they can ever understand) and great friends I overcame the hell I was in and won the war against depression.

My grandpa was the rock I leaned on during these hard times and playing cards with him was the biggest joy of my life. He passed away in April 2012 and there is not a day that goes by that I don't think of him and miss playing cards with him. He was my hero and role model and this book is dedicated to his memory. As he was there for me when I need him the most, I was there for him during his last moments on earth, a fact I wouldn't change for anything. The card playing segment early on in the book is inspired by my card playing with him. Damien losing his grandpa in the book is inspired by the passing of my grandpa. These are the only two events in the book loosely tied to real life events.

I hit rocked bottom in 2010 with depression and that is when I really started getting serious with writing. I have written nonstop since then. It's my love in life and doubt I will ever stop. It has taken awhile for me to reach this moment, but I am finally ready to open up to the world and have everyone read my work.

So here I am publishing my first ever book. This is an exciting moment and I can't wait for everyone to read it. I'm already working on my second book titled The Path Of Evolution. If you are a fan of my work, keep an eye out for that. It will be a poetry book consisting of a lot of poems I have written over the past four years.

You can add me on facebook at www.facebook.com/tyler.zempel or follow me on twitter @tylerzempel. The last two pages of this book I'm leaving blank. It's for you the reader to fill up with notes, ideas, and feelings. Anything you want to put there. If you are fighting depression and want to fight back using writing, use the last pages as your starting point. If you just want to take some notes on the book to understand it better use the last two pages. They are there for you. I thank everyone who buys this book in advance. Thank you very, very much it means a lot to me if you spent your hard earned money on me and support me. I hope you enjoy this book at much as I enjoyed writing it.

I would like to thank the following people personally. My Mom, Dad, brother and my entire family. My Aunt's Fran and Sandy. My Uncle's Scott and Jeff. All four have done a lot for me. My close friends Eric Young, Dave Labar and Casey Wolgast. My girlfriend Kayla Plume for filing a void in my life and bringing peace to my soul. Thank you all very much for all you have done for me.

Lastly, I would like to thank God for giving me this talent and providing me with the strength to share it with the world. I am religious and a believer despite what some people may think reading this book. The book is fiction and doesn't portray my actual belief's.

Tyler Zempel

Dedicated to the memory of Donald Wagner.

I love you and miss you daily. R.I.P.